Get Art Smart

What Is Form?

by Susan Markowitz Meredith

Crabtree Publishing Company

www.crabtreebooks.com

Crabtree Publishing Company

FSC
Mixed Sources
Product group from well-managed forests, controlled sources and recycled wood or fiber
Cert no. SGS-COC-004340
www.fsc.org
© 1996 Forest Stewardship Council

Author: Susan Meredith
Publishing plan research and development:
Sean Charlebois, Reagan Miller
Crabtree Publishing Company
Editors: Reagan Miller
Proofreader: Kathy Middleton, Molly Aloian
Editorial director: Kathy Middleton
Photo research: Edward A. Thomas
Designer: Tammy West, Westgraphix LLC
Production coordinator: Margaret Amy Salter
Prepress technician: Margaret Amy Salter
Consultant: Julie Collins-Dutkiewicz, B.A., specialist in early
childhood education, Sandy Waite, M.Ed., U.S. National
Board Certified Teacher, author, and literacy consultant
Reading Consultant: Susan Nations, M.Ed.,
Author/Literacy Coach/Consultant in Literacy Development

Photographs and reproductions
Cover: Dreamstime; 1: Shutterstock; 5: © Edward A. Thomas; 7, 9, 15: iStockphoto; 11, 17: Private Collection/Photo © Christie's Images/The Bridgeman Art Library; 13: Private Collection/Photo © Boltin Picture Library/The Bridgeman Art Library; 19: Ferens Art Gallery, Hull City Museums and Art Galleries/The Bridgeman Art Library; 21: Private Collection/The Bridgeman Art Library; 23: © F1online digitale Bildagentur GmbH/Alamy.

Front cover (main image): A young artist creates forms in plasticine.
Title page: A young boy holds two apples as an example of form.
Written, developed, and produced by RJF Publishing LLC

Library and Archives Canada Cataloguing in Publication

Meredith, Susan, 1951-
What is form? / Susan Markowitz Meredith.

(Get art smart)
Includes index.
ISBN 978-0-7787-5124-3 (bound).--ISBN 978-0-7787-5138-0 (pbk.)

1. Composition (Art)--Juvenile literature. 2. Form (Aesthetics)--Juvenile
literature. I. Title. II. Series: Get art smart

N7430.M47 2009   j701'.8   C2009-903589-8

Library of Congress Cataloging-in-Publication Data

Meredith, Susan, 1951-

What is form? / Susan Markowitz Meredith.
p. cm. -- (Get art smart)
Includes index.
ISBN 978-0-7787-5138-0 (pbk. : alk. paper) -- ISBN 978-0-7787-5124-3 (reinforced library binding : alk. paper)
1. Composition (Art)--Juvenile literature. 2. Form (Aesthetics)--Juvenile literature. I. Title.

N7430.M42 2009
701'.8--dc22
                    2009023306

Crabtree Publishing Company

www.crabtreebooks.com   1-800-387-7650

Printed in Canada/082010/SO20100728

**Published
in Canada
Crabtree Publishing**
616 Welland Ave.
St. Catharines, Ontario
L2M 5V6

**Published in
the United States
Crabtree Publishing**
PMB 59051
350 Fifth Avenue, 59th Floor
New York, New York 10118

**Published in the
United Kingdom
Crabtree Publishing**
Maritime House
Basin Road North, Hove
BN41 1WR

**Published
in Australia
Crabtree Publishing**
386 Mt. Alexander Rd.
Ascot Vale (Melbourne)
VIC 3032

Contents

What Is Form?

Think of a **square** on a piece of paper. It is a flat shape. We can measure how wide and how tall it is. Now think of a box you can touch. It has a top and a bottom. It has sides all around it, too. We can measure how deep the sides are. A shape that is deep, or thick, is called a **form**.

4

The square on the white paper is flat.
The red box is thick. It is called a form.

5

Flat and Round Sides

Some forms have many flat sides. Other forms are round all over. A ball is a form that is round all over. A **cylinder** has both flat sides and round sides.

 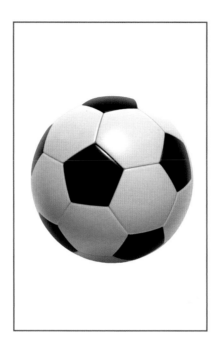 

A refrigerator has flat sides. A soccer ball is round on all sides. A can is a cylinder. It has both round and flat sides.

Forms in Nature

We see forms in nature. Plants and animals are forms that we see in nature. Think of a bird. Its legs are shaped like thin cylinders. Its beak looks like a cone. Its body is curved and very round. Forms in nature often have many parts. Can you find a form with different parts around you?

A bird is a form we see in nature.

Forms We Can Touch

We can make forms when we create art. Sometimes we can make a form out of clay. We can also use wood, stone, metal, and other things to make a form. A form like this is called a **sculpture**. We can walk around many sculptures.

Little Dancer, Aged 14, by Edgar Degas
(1879-1881)

This sculpture is made of metal, wood, and cloth.

Sizes and Parts

Some sculptures are large and heavy. Others are small enough to hold in your hands. These forms may have many parts or just a few. Sometimes we can even add color or lines to sculptures.

Raven totem, by Haida people (1900s)

The lines added to this sculpture help to make the shapes.

13

Forms That Stand Out

There are some sculptures that we cannot walk around. These forms look like they come out of a flat shape. A form like this is called a **relief**. A sculpture on the side of a building is a relief. A picture on a coin is also a relief.

Relief sculpture from Persepolis, Iran, made about 500 B.C.

This relief sculpture was made from rock.

Forms on Paper

We can also make forms on paper. Some artists like to use **brushes**. Some use pens and pencils. These artists use their tools in a special way. On the flat paper, they paint and draw shapes that seem thick. To our eyes, the shapes look like forms.

Surge of Spring, by Emily Carr (early 1900s)

In this painting, the artist made the trees and other shapes look thick.

Forms That Look Real

Some forms on paper look simple. We may use just a few lines to create them. Other forms look more like real objects. Sometimes it takes a long time to make them. Some artists paint their forms on a kind of heavy cloth called **canvas**.

The Lions at Home, by Rosa Bonheur (1881)

In this painting on canvas, the artist made the lions look very real.

Telling a Story

We can share many things with the forms we create. Sometimes forms can tell a story. They may also show animals and people from stories.

Illustration from *Alice in Wonderland*, by John Tenniel (1865)

This picture from *Alice in Wonderland* shows Alice and the Cheshire Cat.

Forms All Around

Look around you. Forms that artists make are everywhere. They are outside on busy streets and in parks. They are inside buildings, too. Some forms are on paper or canvas. Some are sculptures. Each form says something special. What forms have you seen?

Martin Luther King, Jr., by Lisa Reinertson (1999)

This sculpture of Martin Luther King, Jr. is outside in Riverside, California.

23

Words to Know

brushes

canvas

cylinder

thick
shape

form

relief

sculpture

square

Find Out More

Books

Johnson, Stephen T. *A Is for Art: An Abstract Alphabet*. New York: Simon & Schuster/Paula Wiseman Books, 2008.

Scieszka, Jon. *Seen Art?* New York: Scholastic, 2005.

Web sites

Haring Kids: art games and activities
www.haringkids.com

Lizzy and Gordon Visit the Sculpture Garden
www.nga.gov/kids/lizzy/lizzy.htm